Diane Abbott Biography Book

The Untold Story of Britain's First Black Female MP

By

Carlos Hummell

Copyright © 2024 [Carlos Hummell]. All rights reserved. This work is protected by copyright law and may not be reproduced, distributed, transmitted, displayed, published, or broadcast without the prior written permission of the copyright owner. You may not alter or remove any trademark, copyright, or other notice from copies of the content. Unauthorized use and/or duplication of this material without express and written permission from the copyright owner is strictly prohibited. Excerpts and links may be used, provided that full and clear credit is given to [Carlos Hummell] with appropriate and specific direction to the original content.

TABLE OF CONTENTS

Copyright

TABLE OF CONTENTS

INTRODUCTION

CHAPTER ONE

   Early Life and Family Roots

CHAPTER TWO

   The Making of a Political Mind

CHAPTER THREE

   Breaking Barriers in British Politics

CHAPTER FOUR

   Advocacy and Impact in Parliament

CHAPTER FIVE

   Diane Abbott as Shadow Home Secretary

CONCLUSION

INTRODUCTION

Diane Abbott is a name that reverberates through the corridors of British political history, a name synonymous with breaking barriers and standing firm in the face of adversity. As the first Black woman ever elected to the House of Commons in the United Kingdom, Diane Abbott has charted an extraordinary course, not just for herself but for generations of politicians, activists, and citizens inspired by her trailblazing journey. This biography seeks to uncover the many layers of Abbott's life — the struggles and triumphs, the personal and political, the public service and the private battles — to tell the untold story of one of Britain's most compelling and resilient political figures.

Diane Abbott's life story begins in the heart of London, where she was born in Paddington on September 27, 1953, to Jamaican immigrant parents. Her father was a welder, and her mother was a nurse, both having come to Britain as part of the Windrush generation seeking better opportunities in a country that promised prosperity after the Second World War. The young Diane grew up in a working-class household that prized education and hard work as the keys to success in a society where racial prejudice was a stark reality. Her parents instilled in her a strong sense of justice and a determination to make a difference, values that would shape her entire life.

Diane Abbott's early education at Harrow County Grammar School was a defining period that exposed her to both the privileges and prejudices of British society. As one of the few Black students in a predominantly white environment, she experienced firsthand the casual racism and discrimination that would become a recurring theme in her life. Yet, it was here that her passion for learning flourished. Abbott excelled academically and displayed an early interest in politics, particularly in issues concerning race, equality, and social justice. This interest deepened during her time at Newnham College, Cambridge, where she read History, becoming one of only a handful of Black women at the university in the early 1970s. Her years at Cambridge were marked by intellectual rigor and a growing political consciousness shaped by the civil rights movements in the United States and the anti-apartheid struggle in South Africa.

After graduating from Cambridge, Abbott embarked on a career that combined public service and media. She began working as a civil servant in the Home Office, where she was involved in immigration policy, an experience that opened her eyes to the systemic inequalities within British institutions. Her time at the Home Office was pivotal in shaping her views on race and immigration, issues she would later champion in Parliament. From there, she moved into journalism, working as a reporter and researcher for Thames Television and as a public relations officer at the Greater London Council, where she became known for her eloquence and persuasive advocacy on behalf of marginalized communities.

In 1987, Abbott's life took a historic turn when she was elected as the Member of Parliament for Hackney North and Stoke Newington, a moment that marked the beginning of a political career defined by firsts. Her election was part of a wave that saw the entry of four Black and Asian MPs into the House of Commons — Bernie Grant, Paul Boateng, Keith Vaz, and Abbott herself — forever altering the landscape of British politics. Diane Abbott's victory was not just a personal achievement but a watershed moment for the UK, a sign that Parliament, long a bastion of white male privilege, was beginning to open its doors to a more diverse range of voices.

Abbott's entry into Parliament was both historic and groundbreaking, but it was not without challenges. From the very beginning, she faced hostility, both overt and covert, from within the political establishment and the media. As a Black woman in a predominantly white, male-dominated institution, she was frequently subjected to racist and sexist abuse, often criticized not just for her policies and views but for her very presence. Despite these obstacles, Abbott refused to be silenced or sidelined. She quickly established herself as a fearless advocate for her constituents and a vocal critic of injustice, inequality, and institutional racism.

Over the years, Abbott has built a reputation as one of the most outspoken and principled members of Parliament, known for her willingness to take unpopular stands and speak truth to power. She has been a consistent advocate for education, healthcare, and social justice, often highlighting the impact of government policies on the most vulnerable in society. She has championed issues such as police reform, housing, mental health, and civil liberties, and has been a relentless critic of the austerity measures that have disproportionately affected the poor and marginalized communities. Her work has always been driven by a deep-seated belief in fairness and equality, a commitment to social justice that was instilled in her from an early age.

Perhaps one of the most defining periods of Abbott's career came when she was appointed as Shadow Home Secretary in 2016, under the leadership of Jeremy Corbyn. As Shadow Home Secretary, she was responsible for shaping the Labour Party's policies on crucial issues such as immigration, policing, and national security. Abbott used this platform to push for progressive policies that aimed at reforming the criminal justice system, protecting civil liberties, and challenging the xenophobia that had become increasingly prevalent in British politics in the wake of Brexit. Her tenure as Shadow Home Secretary was marked by both significant policy contributions and personal challenges, including health battles and relentless attacks from political opponents and the media.

Yet, Diane Abbott's legacy goes beyond her policy positions and political roles. She is also a symbol of resilience and perseverance in the face of adversity. Throughout her career, she has faced an onslaught of racist and sexist abuse, becoming one of the most targeted MPs on social media. But rather than retreating into silence, Abbott has used her experiences to highlight the pervasive nature of discrimination in society and to advocate for greater protection against hate speech and harassment. Her courage in the face of such attacks has inspired countless individuals, especially women and people of color, to enter public life and fight for a more just and inclusive society.

In addition to her political achievements, Abbott has been a tireless advocate for public health and education, recognizing the critical importance of these issues in creating a fairer society. Her commitment to these causes is deeply personal. As a single mother raising her son, James, she has spoken openly about the challenges of balancing a demanding political career with parenthood and the unique pressures faced by Black mothers in Britain. Her experiences as a mother have informed her approach to policy, particularly in advocating for better childcare, educational opportunities, and support for single-parent families.

Despite her long and distinguished career, Diane Abbott remains a polarizing figure in British politics. Her critics often accuse her of being too radical, too outspoken, or too uncompromising. Yet her supporters view her as a voice of conscience in a political landscape that too often prioritizes expedience over principle. What is undeniable is her impact: as a pioneer for women and minorities in politics, as a champion of social justice, and as a steadfast advocate for those who have been marginalized by the systems of power.

This biography aims to delve into the complexities of Diane Abbott's life and career, to tell the story of a woman who has broken through countless barriers, faced down seemingly insurmountable challenges, and remained unwavering in her commitment to justice and equality. It seeks to paint a full picture of her achievements and her struggles, to explore the moments that defined her, and to offer a deeper understanding of her influence on British politics and society.

Diane Abbott's story is not just a tale of political success; it is a narrative of resilience, courage, and hope. It is a reminder that the fight for justice and equality is ongoing, that progress is often slow and hard-won, and that every voice raised against injustice adds to the chorus demanding change. Through this book, we celebrate the untold story of Britain's first Black female MP, a woman who has changed the face of British politics and who continues to inspire new generations to take up the mantle of leadership and fight for a fairer, more inclusive world.

CHAPTER ONE

Early Life and Family Roots

Diane Abbott was born on September 27, 1953, in Paddington, West London, an area known for its diverse population and historic railway station. Her arrival came at a time when London was suffering with postwar recovery, social transition, and the first wave of large-scale immigration from Commonwealth countries, particularly Jamaica, where her parents had migrated. The young Abbott's early years in Paddington were full of adventure, turmoil, and progress.

Diane was in Paddington and witnessed a stunning tapestry of multicultural London life. Her area was bustling yet sometimes tough for a young Black girl. London in the 1950s and 1960s was a metropolis whose communities were still adjusting to new cultural dynamics, posing both opportunities and challenges for people of color. Diane's family lived in a small flat, as did many other immigrants who had come to Britain looking for better opportunities but were often working in low-wage jobs. Diane's father was a welder, a physically demanding occupation, and her mother was a nurse who worked long hours for the healthcare system. They had both dropped out of school at the age of 14, but they believed that education and hard work could transform their lives.

Diane considered Paddington as more than just a neighborhood; it was the setting for her formative years, during which she developed her worldview and sense of self. Her parents instilled in her a strong sense of discipline and a desire for academic accomplishment, both of which would aid her ascent to political prominence. She attended Harrow County Grammar School, where she was often one of the few Black students in her class. This interaction taught her about the challenges of entering predominantly white environments where she had to constantly demonstrate her existence and importance.

Diane Abbott's story is deeply related to her Jamaican heritage. Her parents, part of the "Windrush Generation," immigrated to the United Kingdom in the early 1950s, carrying with them the hopes and goals of many Caribbean people. At the time, Jamaica was still a British colony, and many Jamaicans saw the "Mother Country" as a land of opportunity, where they could start again with their families.

Diane's father was a proud and hardworking guy who left Jamaica to make a better life for his children. As a welder, he worked hard at a job that demanded both talent and physical endurance. He was frequently out from home, working late, yet he remained an important part of Diane's life. His drive to care for his family was matched by a calm dignity and a strong belief in fairness and justice, which he hoped to impart in his daughter. Diane often recalls Michael's descriptions of Jamaica, which included lush green hills, lively music, and a strong sense of community. These legends instilled in her a deep sense of pride in her history, which she kept with her throughout her life.

Her mother, a strong and kind nurse, exercised equal authority. Like many women of her generation, she balanced the demands of a busy job with the responsibilities of raising a family. Diane's mother was a source of strength and resilience; she never shied away from difficult tasks and taught her the importance of compassion, perseverance, and persistence. Despite the pressures of her job, Diane's mother always found time for her family, reading to her and encouraged her to follow her aspirations.

Diane's parents dropped out of school when they were 14 years old, which was common in Jamaica at the time due to financial restrictions and a lack of access to secondary education. They focused on giving their daughter opportunities that they did not have. They viewed education as the key to breaking the cycle of poverty and injustice, thus they emphasized Diane's academic successes. This commitment reflected not only personal desire, but also a greater struggle for equality and recognition in a culture that had saw Black people as second-class citizens.

Diane's Jamaican heritage also shaped her views. She grew up around Jamaican storytelling, music, and culture. Her parents communicated to her in Jamaican Patois, a language rich in history and passion, and she grew up listening to reggae, calypso, and ska music that conveyed messages of resilience, tenacity, and hope. These cultural characteristics were more than just a way of life; they reflected Diane's connection to a larger diasporic identity, linking her to a global network of individuals of African descent who had survived colonization, migration, and the civil rights movement.

Diane Abbott began her education at a local primary school, where she quickly shown an aptitude for learning. Her teachers commended her interest and ability to absorb complex information, and she consistently outperformed her peers in courses like history and English. Diane was not only an exceptional student, but also a voracious reader, devouring novels that transported her to new realms and fueled her imagination. Diane discovered a love of literature during these formative years, which she has kept with her throughout her life.

Diane demonstrated an early interest in politics and social justice. She would listen closely to her parents' comments about the challenges that immigrants face in Britain, as well as the injustices that colonial power produced in Jamaica. These chats inspired her to become an activist, challenging the existing quo and working toward a more fair society. Diane grew aware of injustices in her school and community, prompting her to ask why things were the way they were. Her parents encouraged her curiosity, honed her intellect, and helped her develop a strong moral compass.

Diane was accepted into Harrow County Grammar School, one of the area's most well-known grammar schools, when she was ready to begin secondary school. Harrow delivers a challenging academic and social environment. Diane found herself as one of the few Black students at a predominantly white university, and the experience left an indelible impression on her. She faced discrimination and hatred from both students and professors, but instead of giving up, she became more determined to succeed.

Diane excelled in her studies at Harrow, particularly history and English, allowing her to understand and comprehend the complexities of her surroundings. She was a dedicated student who spent countless hours in the library researching social movements, civil rights, and political ideologies. She also improved her public speaking skills by participating in debates and discussions, which would later help her political career.

Diane's early objectives were shaped by the political and social milieu of the 1960s and 1970s, a time of great upheaval and change. The civil rights movement in the United States, the anti-apartheid struggle in South Africa, and the decolonization of African and Caribbean countries piqued her curiosity and motivated her to make a difference. Martin Luther King Jr., Malcolm X, and Nelson Mandela were among those who motivated her to speak out against injustice and inequality.

Despite these hurdles, Diane excelled at Harrow County Grammar School. She was desperate to demonstrate her worth, both to those who questioned her and to herself. Her parents' difficulties, the travel from Jamaica to Britain, hard work, and belief in the need of education all aided her success. She recognized that her accomplishment would be a reflection of their efforts and an opportunity to fulfill their goals.

Diane Abbott then attended Newnham Institution in Cambridge, a women's college associated with the University of Cambridge. Her admission to Cambridge was a significant success not only for her, but also for her family and community. It illustrated that, despite the obstacles, a young Black lady from a working-class immigrant family could rise to the summit of British intellectual achievement. Diane studied history at Cambridge, which gave her the opportunity to delve extensively into the issues of race, class, and power that had always captivated her interest.

For Diane, Cambridge was both a difficulty and an opportunity. It was a place where she was subjected to unrivaled scrutiny, where she was occasionally the only Black student in her classes, and where she was always expected to demonstrate her academic abilities. It was also when she found her voice, debated race and gender issues, and formed her opinions on social justice and equality.

Diane became highly involved in student politics at Cambridge after joining the Cambridge Union, the university's well-known debating group. She used this platform to speak out against racism, sexism, and other forms of discrimination, honing her oratorical skills and gaining confidence in her ability to lead and persuade. It was here that she first explored a career in public service, realizing that she might use her voice and education to effect change.

After graduating from Cambridge, Diane worked as a civil servant in the Home Office, where she gained direct experience with government operations.

However, she quickly realized that her true love was elsewhere. She went on to work as a journalist, first for Thames Television and later for the Morning Star, a left-wing daily, where she continued to speak out against racism, inequality, and social justice. Her writing was powerful and unyielding, challenging the status quo and advocating for the rights of the poor and underprivileged.

Her early career decisions were about more than just obtaining work; they were also about creating a platform from which she could fight the injustices she saw around her. Diane realized that in order to make a big difference, she needed to be able to speak up and influence legislation and public opinion. This epiphany pushed her into politics, where she could combine her passion for social justice with a desire to help her community.

Diane Abbott, an experienced campaigner and advocate, chose to run for Parliament in 1987. She was well aware of the problems confronting her community, and she had a clear vision of the type of society she wished to contribute to. Her upbringing in London, Jamaican heritage, education, and early career all prepared her for the challenges that were ahead. They had given her the self-assurance, fortitude, and determination required to become Britain's first Black female MP, breaking down boundaries and opening the way for future generations of Black and minority leaders.

Diane Abbott's childhood and family history highlight the power of perseverance, the value of education, and the importance of cultural heritage. They tell the story of a little girl who, despite the hurdles, chose to dream big and refused to be defined by the limitations that others put on her. It's a story about determination, bravery, and the unwavering belief that one person can make a difference.

CHAPTER TWO

The Making of a Political Mind

Diane Abbott's rise to fame as one of the UK's most well-known and progressive politicians began years before her historic election to Parliament in 1987. It's a story of perseverance, determination, and unrelenting dedication to social justice, inspired by her upbringing in London and professional experiences. From her education at prestigious institutions to her multiple professional roles, Abbott cultivated a political mind acutely aware of societal inequities and challenges, particularly those affecting race, gender, and class.

Diane Abbott started her education at Harrow County School for Girls, a grammar school in London, where she set the groundwork for her future political career. As a young student in the 1960s, Abbott encountered a challenging educational environment that was not always welcoming to students of color. Abbott displayed a voracious mind and a desire to learn early in her political career.

Her time at Harrow County was marked by a deep interest in history and a desire to understand the bigger forces that govern the world. She excelled intellectually, but more importantly, she became aware of current social issues, such as the treatment of people of African and Caribbean descent in Britain. Abbott's first introduction to the complexities of British society was in school, where she sharpened her critical thinking skills and capacity to join in heated arguments.

Despite the social and ethnic challenges she faced, Abbott was encouraged and supported by several of her instructors, who recognized her abilities and assisted her in achieving her goals. A mix of personal effort, academic interest, and assistance led her to Cambridge, one of the world's most prestigious universities.

Diane Abbott's admission to Newnham College, Cambridge, in the early 1970s was a watershed moment not only for her but also for the United Kingdom, as few Black students, particularly Black women, attended renowned colleges at the time. She studied history at Cambridge, where she discovered the intertwining stories of power, empire, and resistance that would define her political views.

Abbott's experience at Cambridge was both inspiring and stressful. As one of the university's few Black women, she was routinely subjected to various forms of discrimination. The academic environment was difficult, and she had to deal with both the demands of a tough curriculum and the subtle, but often overt, racism of her students and instructors. Despite these challenges, Abbott exhibited her academic potential by receiving a lower second-class degree (2:2) in history. One of her supervisors was Simon Schama, a now-famous historian who was a young professor just getting started.

Abbott conducted study under Schama's direction on issues ranging from the history of the British Empire to the political movements that defined the twentieth century. These studies shaped her understanding of the historical roots of socioeconomic inequality, as well as the long-term consequences of colonialism and racism. Her time at Cambridge was about more than just academic achievement; she met new people and was exposed to a wide variety of ideas and perspectives, all of which informed her political thinking.

After graduating from Cambridge in 1973, Abbott began a complex career that reflected her diverse interests and growing commitment to social justice. Her first job was as an administrative trainee at the Home Office from 1976 to 1978. This employment provided her with an inside look at how the government operates and the bureaucratic processes that shape UK policy and administration. Her time at the Home Office gave her firsthand knowledge of how top-level decisions were made and how they affected ordinary people, particularly marginalized communities. It also introduced her to structural difficulties in government, particularly those involving race relations and social policy.

From 1978 to 1980, Abbott was a Race Relations Officer with the National Council for Civil Liberties (now

Liberty), where he focused on civil rights and discrimination issues. This position became a turning event in her career, allowing her to actively engage with community organizations and advocate for minority rights. It was here that she discovered her voice as a social justice champion, as well as the importance of grassroots activism and the art of negotiation.

Abbott began his media career in 1980 as a researcher and reporter for Thames Television, a popular broadcaster at the time. From 1980 to 1983, she covered a wide range of social and political issues for Thames Television, providing a unique perspective to the newsroom. Her work at Thames Television allowed her to bring to light issues that had previously gone undetected by the mainstream media, particularly those affecting Black communities and other underprivileged groups.

After leaving Thames Television, Abbott worked as a researcher for TV-am, a breakfast television network, between 1983 and 1985. This job enabled her to improve her communication skills and get a better understanding of how the media influences public opinion and policy. During his time in journalism, Abbott understood the potential for political change through both media coverage and active political action.

In 1985, Abbott began working as a Press Officer for the Greater London Council (GLC), where he reported to Ken Livingstone, a prominent Marxist politician. She was in the heart of London's radical political movement, spearheading battles against government policies on housing, education, and race relations. Her responsibilities include managing the GLC's media relations and public messaging, which provides her with unique insights into political strategy and communication.

From 1986 to 1987, she was the Head of Press and Public Relations for Lambeth Council, one of London's most diverse and politically active boroughs. She managed the council's public image during a period of significant social and political change. These experiences solidified her image as a steadfast advocate for social justice and laid the groundwork for her future political career.

Abbott was placed under official monitoring in the 1980s as a result of her acts. During the 2024 Undercover Policing Inquiry, it was found that the Metropolitan Police used undercover officers to eavesdrop on anti-racist activists such as Abbott. Secret police documents detail her activities, revealing the state's suspicion and surveillance of Black activists and organizations striving for civil rights and social justice. Abbott condemned these behaviors as discriminatory and unacceptable, highlighting the ongoing fight against systemic racism in British culture.

Abbott began her professional political career in 1982, when she was elected to the Westminster City Council, where she served until 1986. During her time on the council, she grew more active in internal Labour Party politics and local concerns. In 1983, she was an important figure in the Labour Party's Black Sections movement, alongside well-known Black MPs such as Bernie Grant, Paul Boateng, and Keith Vaz. This movement aimed to increase Black and Asian representation in the Labour Party, ensuring that their views were heard and stated.

Despite internal criticism, Abbott pushed for greater diversity inside the party. She campaigned as a Labour candidate for Brent East in 1985, but was beaten by Ken Livingstone. This failure did not discourage her; rather, it fueled her determination to fight for representation and social justice, paving the path for her historic election to Parliament in 1987.

Several events shaped Diane Abbott's early life and career, helping her to become the tough, outspoken, and influential politician she is today. Abbott's commitment to fairness, justice, and representation began at Harrow County School for Girls and Newnham College in Cambridge, and has continued throughout her early careers in civil service, journalism, and local government. These formative years helped shape her political perspective, which would eventually challenge the status quo and inspire subsequent generations of politicians and activists in the United Kingdom and around the world.

CHAPTER THREE

Breaking Barriers in British Politics

Diane Abbott entered politics with a clear sense of purpose and a strong desire to make a change. In 1987, she became the first black woman elected to the United Kingdom's House of Commons. This election was more than just a political milestone; it signaled a watershed moment in the fight for representation and equality in British politics. Abbott ran as the Labour Party's candidate in Hackney North and Stoke Newington, a diverse East London neighbourhood, and won by 48.7%, or 7,678 votes.

Her triumph in the 1987 general election was groundbreaking. Abbott's triumph sparked a political revolution, upsetting the established order and reflecting a nation in transition. It was the result of years of effort, agitation, and belief in a more inclusive political strategy. Her success was underlined by the fact that she was the first Black woman admitted to a prestigious university dominated by white men. Her candidacy was not without challenges, including discrimination, skepticism, and an often hostile media environment toward the concept of a Black female MP.

Diane Abbott's election as the country's first black female MP was a watershed moment in British politics, addressing racial and gender disparities. Her very presence challenged long-held beliefs and paved the way for future generations of underrepresented politicians. Abbott's victory was more than just personal; it signaled the rise of social justice organizations and hard-fought campaigns for representation.

Abbott, Britain's first Black female MP, became a symbol of opportunity and progress. She represented a minority that has traditionally been underrepresented in positions of power. Her win conveyed a clear message: Britain's political environment was beginning to reflect its own diversity. Abbott's search, however, was not only symbolic; it had real consequences. She started utilizing her platform to advocate social justice, racial harmony, and equality. She became a voice for the oppressed, lobbying for legislation to alleviate structural inequalities and highlight the problems that her community faces.

Diane Abbott's campaign faced various challenges. She was met with harsh criticism and hatred from the start. The British media was frequently hostile, and some politicians questioned her legitimacy and competence.

Racism and sexism were recurrent undercurrents that sought to undermine her integrity and ambition for public office. Nonetheless, Abbott remained resolute. She worked hard on her campaign, visiting communities, talking about local issues, and underlining the need for greater representation and justice in British politics.

Her accomplishments included not only earning the seat, but also overcoming obstacles and displaying tenacity in the face of hardship. Abbott's victory in the 1987 election laid the groundwork for future minority candidates. It was a win for everyone who believed in the principles of equality and democracy.

Abbott won the 1987 Hackney North and Stoke Newington MP election with 7,678 votes (48.7%). Her election kicked off a long and successful career in the House of Commons, where she continued to break down barriers and agitate for reform. Abbott's ability to traverse a predominantly white and male-dominated political system demonstrated her political savvy, ambition, and unwavering dedication to her values.

Following her election, Abbott rapidly established herself as a strong member of Parliament. She worked on several legislative committees that addressed both domestic and international issues. Abbott held numerous shadow cabinet positions in subsequent Shadow Cabinets, indicating her rising status within the Labour Party. She worked on the Treasury Select Committee in the 1990s, where she researched economic policies and fought for fiscal fairness and social justice.

Later, Abbott worked on the Foreign Affairs Select Committee, where she investigated delicate international matters such as human rights and foreign policy. Despite being a minority voice, her selection for these positions demonstrated her dedication to being a constructive and critical member of Parliament who is not hesitant to raise difficult subjects or contradict popular opinion.

Abbott's parliamentary responsibility extended beyond committee work. She also made tremendous progress in advancing civil liberties. Her argument during the 2008 Counter-Terrorism Bill discussion was so compelling that it received The Spectator magazine's "Parliamentary Speech of the Year" award, as well as special mention at the 2008 Human Rights Awards. Abbott's statements regularly stressed both her people' concerns and larger societal challenges, combining academic rigor and emotional appeal.

Diane Abbott's political career has been defined by numerous re-elections, demonstrating her continuous popularity and supporters' trust in her. In 1992, Abbott was reelected with a 57.8% increase in votes and a 10,727 majority. This trend continued in the 1997 general election, when her vote share increased to 65.2%, resulting in a comfortable margin of 15,627 votes. Her successful re-election campaigns indicated her growing influence in her constituency and the Labour Party, as well as her ability to interact with a wide range of voters.

Despite setbacks, Abbott displayed political tenacity by holding onto her post in subsequent elections. In the

2001 general election, she won with 61% of the vote and a majority of 13,651. She won reelection in 2005 with 48.6% of the vote and a 7,427-vote margin. Abbott's fluctuating vote share throughout the years reflected the changing dynamics of her neighborhood and the greater political scene, but she remained a strong advocate of her community.

Abbott's influence in Parliament grew, and she presided over several All-Party Parliamentary Groups, including the British-Caribbean Group and the Sickle Cell and Thalassemia Group. Her work extended beyond the parliamentary floor, as she established the London Schools and the Black Child initiative, which aimed to enhance educational outcomes for Black children. This attempt illustrates her dedication to combating systemic injustices and advocating for marginalized individuals.

Diane Abbott's influence on British politics has been extensively acknowledged. Goldsmiths' College conducted a jubilee ceremony in 2012 to commemorate her 25th year in Parliament. Notable speakers at the occasion included Herman Ouseley, Linton Kwesi Johnson, and Shami Chakrabarti, all of whom lauded Abbott's political passion and pioneering position. Her accomplishments were hailed not only as personal milestones, but also as a symbol of progress for marginalized groups in British society.

Abbott's long-term political success was demonstrated in the 2015 general election, when she won re-election with 62.9% of the vote and a 24,008 margin. In the

2017 snap general election, she won 75.1% of the vote, a historic majority of 35,139. Her ability to sustain and even enhance her support over time showed her tight relationship with her constituents and the respect she earned from all sides of the political aisle.

Abbott's remarks at a House of Commons discussion on the Caribbean were later included in Margaret Busby's 2019 book, "New Daughters of Africa," demonstrating her significance in modern political discourse.

Diane Abbott's career continued to grow. In the 2019 general election, she was re-elected with a 70.3% vote share and a 33,188 majority, cementing her place as a crucial actor in British politics. Even in the 2024 general election, she was reelected with 60% of the vote, demonstrating her continued relevance and influence.

Abbott received the symbolic title "Mother of the House," which recognizes her as the longest-serving female MP. On July 9, 2024, she delivered her first address in this role, congratulating new MPs and reflecting on women's success in Parliament, highlighting the importance of equality and diversity in political participation.

Her address focused on developments in Parliament since she took office in 1987, noting a rise in the number of female MPs from forty to 264. Abbott thanked her predecessor, Baroness Harriet Harman, for her ongoing efforts to make the House of Commons more inclusive and representative. Speaker of the House of Commons Sir Lindsay Hoyle and Prime Minister Keir Starmer both lauded Abbott's efforts, describing her as a trailblazer and campaigner for social fairness.

Diane Abbott's rise in British politics has been nothing short of transformational. From her historic election in 1987 as Britain's first Black female MP to her current position as "Mother of the House," she has continuously pushed boundaries, questioned the status quo, and inspired many others to follow in her footsteps. Her persistence, commitment to justice, and advocacy for underprivileged communities have catapulted her to the forefront of Britain's ongoing equality struggle. Abbott's narrative is one of courage, tenacity, and steadfast commitment to public service, cementing her legacy as a trailblazer and pioneer for future generations.

CHAPTER FOUR

Advocacy and Impact in Parliament

Diane Abbott has made significant contributions to British politics, using her position in Parliament to promote social justice, education, and healthcare reform. Throughout her career, she has been a vocal supporter of progressive policies that benefit marginalized areas. Abbott, the first Black female Member of Parliament (MP) in the United Kingdom, has faced and overcome significant challenges, cementing her reputation as a trailblazer and passionate advocate for advancement.

Abbott's main areas of advocacy in Parliament have been education and healthcare. Recognizing the importance of these sectors in creating equitable opportunities for all, she has long fought for policies that reduce inequality and improve access to high-quality services.

In education, Abbott is a staunch advocate of comprehensive education and has spoken out against privatization and the introduction of market forces into the education system. She has attacked the academy school model, stating that it exacerbates inequality by creating a two-tier system in which some students obtain a higher education than others. Instead, she has fought for increased public school financing, better teacher pay and working conditions, and more inclusive educational policies that meet the needs of all children, regardless of socioeconomic position.

Abbott has also been a strong champion for healthcare reform, particularly within the National Health Service (NHS). She has campaigned for increased NHS funding while warning about the dangers of privatization and commercial interests in public healthcare. As Shadow Minister for Public Health, she was in charge of issues like children's health, maternity care, sexual health, tobacco control, nursing, obesity, and alcohol addiction. During her time in this position, she became an outspoken opponent of austerity measures that threatened the NHS, arguing that healthcare should be available to everyone, not just those who can pay it. Her contributions to this issue were widely recognized, with The Telegraph describing her in 2011 as "one of Labour's best front bench performers."

Abbott's advocacy extends beyond education and healthcare to address greater issues of racial and social justice. As a Black woman in a predominantly white Parliament, she has long led the charge against racism, sexism, and other forms of discrimination. She has actively advocated for equal rights, opposing police violence, racial profiling, and discriminatory immigration policies.

One of her most important achievements in this field was her participation in the campaign against police "stop and search" powers, which have been accused of unfairly targeting Black and minority ethnic groups. Abbott has supported for increased accountability and transparency in the use of these authorities, as well as modifications to reduce their discriminatory impact.

Abbott has also used her platform to oppose the hostile environment policy toward immigrants, stating that it fosters intolerance and xenophobia while causing undue hardship for vulnerable people. She has pushed for the rights of refugees and asylum seekers, as well as a more compassionate immigration policy that respects everyone's humanity and dignity.

Throughout her political career, Abbott has backed the Labour Party's left side. She has been a prominent member of the party's progressive wing, advocating for public ownership of key corporations, an end to austerity measures, and a more redistributive tax structure. Abbott's policies are based on his belief in social justice, equality, and the government's ability to contribute to a more equitable society.

Abbott announced her candidacy for Labour leadership on May 20, 2010, after Gordon Brown resigned as party leader. Despite being viewed as an underdog during the campaign, she was able to secure the necessary 33 nominations, thanks in part to John McDonnell's resignation and the support of David Miliband and Jack Straw. Despite losing the first round of voting by 7.24%, her campaign was notable for demonstrating the power and influence of the party's left-wing factions.

Following the leadership contest, the new Labour leader, Ed Miliband, appointed Abbott as Shadow Minister of Public Health. In this position, she shadowed a variety of public health issues, including children's health, maternity care, sexual health, tobacco, nursing, obesity, and alcoholism. Her performance in this job was widely praised, with The Telegraph calling her "one of Labour's best front-bench performers."

Abbott became a vocal "pro-choice" abortion supporter, fighting changes in abortion counseling standards and time constraints. She left a cross-party abortion counseling group, stating it was a cover for anti-abortion organizations seeking to limit reproductive rights without an open debate in Parliament. Abbott's firm stance on this issue solidified her reputation as a staunch supporter of women's rights and reproductive freedom.

In 2011, Abbott voted in favor of military intervention in Libya, displaying her willingness to consider a range of foreign policy options that aligned with her convictions. On February 5, 2013, she voted in favor of the Marriage (Same Sex Couples) Bill, confirming her commitment to equality and LGBTQ rights.

On October 8, 2013, Ed Miliband, Labour leader, appointed Luciana Berger as Shadow Public Health Minister, following Abbott. Many interpreted this decision as part of Miliband's greater attempt to centralize the Labour Party, which has occasionally resulted in the marginalization of its more left-wing members. Despite his defeat, Abbott stayed involved in politics.

Abbott showed an interest in running for Mayor of London in 2016, and on November 30, 2014, she announced her desire to run as Labour's candidate. In 2015, she did not receive the nomination. Despite her defeat, her willingness to seek for such a prestigious post demonstrated her ongoing commitment to public service and desire to make a difference in local government.

In January 2015, she was one of 16 people who signed an open letter to Ed Miliband, encouraging the party to take a stronger stance against austerity, commit to returning rail franchises to public ownership, and strengthen collective bargaining. This choice demonstrated her dedication to the Labour Party's more radical aspects, as well as her continuous advocacy for policies that promote social justice and economic fairness.

CHAPTER FIVE

Diane Abbott as Shadow Home Secretary

Diane Abbott, a veteran British Labour politician, was Shadow Home Secretary from October 2016 to April 2020. Abbott has long held significant power in the Labour Party and British politics, most notably as a close ally of Jeremy Corbyn. Her stint in this position was distinguished by her advocacy for progressive issues, her handling of harsh scrutiny and controversy, and her unflinching commitment to Corbyn's leadership vision. The sections that follow delve into her fundamental beliefs and points of view, how she handled criticism, her involvement throughout the Corbyn era, and watershed moments in her political career.

Diane Abbott held numerous significant positions as Shadow Home Secretary, displaying her long-standing dedication to social justice, equality, and civil liberties. Here are some of her main policy positions:

Policing and Crime: Abbott advocated for a more community-focused approach to policing, highlighting the importance of trust between officers and the communities they serve. She was a prominent opponent of austerity-driven cuts to police spending and advocated for the recruitment of more officers, particularly those from minority backgrounds, to better reflect the diversity of British society. Despite criticism for how she handled the proposal's financial challenges, she supported Labour's vow to hire 10,000 extra police officers to improve public safety in the 2017 general election.

Immigration and asylum: Abbott advocated for a more egalitarian and humane immigration system, frequently criticizing the Conservative government's "hostile environment" policy. She advocated for the rights of refugees and asylum seekers, proposing more humanitarian policies for those escaping conflict and persecution. She also spoke out against deportations and denounced the UK government's Windrush affair, in which British residents were wrongfully held, denied legal rights, and deported.

Abbott was well-known for her uncompromising commitment to civil liberties and human rights. She was always opposed to policies that she saw as overly wide in terms of monitoring and state control. She was against ID cards and government intrusions into people's private. Her voting record included opposition to renewing Britain's Trident nuclear weapons and support for amendments extending abortion rights, notably in Northern Ireland.

Racial Justice and Equality: Abbott, who became the first Black woman elected to the House of Commons in 1987, has long pushed for racial justice and equality. She spoke out against the systemic disadvantages that ethnic minority communities in the United Kingdom endure, and she advocated for changes to address disparities in education, health, employment, and criminal justice.

Diane Abbott's stint as Shadow Home Secretary was distinguished by a number of high-profile episodes that drew widespread media coverage. These issues were typically founded on alleged blunders in interviews or utterances about sensitive topics.

2017 General Election Campaign Gaffes: During the 2017 general election campaign, Abbott made several questionable media appearances. In an interview with LBC Radio on May 2, 2017, she struggled to provide an exact amount for Labour's vow to hire 10,000 more police officers. The performance was largely perceived as a "car crash," with Labour leader Jeremy Corbyn later congratulating her and claiming he was not embarrassed by the interview. Additional interviews, including one with ITV on May 5, 2017, revealed more concerns with number display. Critics and political opponents used these episodes to highlight her perceived unfitness for office.

Position on Terrorism and Security: Abbott has faced criticism for her previous statements and positions on security and counterterrorism. During an interview with the BBC's "Andrew Marr Show" in May 2017, she was asked about her apparent sympathy for the Irish Republican Army (IRA) in the early 1980s, as well as her previous support for the elimination of MI5 and Special Branch. She pointed out that the restrictions were imposed decades ago, and that both corporations have since made considerable modifications.

Handling of the Harris Report: On June 5, 2017, Abbott appeared on Sky News but was unable to respond to questions on the Harris report on defending London from terrorist attacks. Despite her claim to have read the booklet, she couldn't remember any of the 127 subjects. This incident showed how she struggled with her role. The next day, she was unable to participate in a joint interview with Amber Rudd on "Woman's Hour" due to illness. Later, it was revealed that Abbott was receiving treatment for type 2 diabetes, which she was diagnosed with in 2015, and that the election campaign's stress and pace had harmed her health.

Diane Abbott was a key ally of Jeremy Corbyn during his time as Labour Party leader. Her support for Corbyn and similar political principles affected her tenure as Shadow Home Secretary.

Abbott was one of 36 Labour MPs that nominated Jeremy Corbyn for the 2015 leadership election. Following his triumph, she was named Shadow Secretary of State for International Development. Following a succession of resignations from Corbyn's shadow cabinet in 2016, she was elevated to Shadow Health Secretary before being appointed Shadow Home Secretary in October 2016. Despite fierce criticism from the Labour Party and the larger political establishment, Abbott remained resolutely loyal to Corbyn throughout his tenure.

Obstacles in the Role: As a major member of Corbyn's shadow cabinet, Abbott faced a number of problems, including party unity, media scrutiny, and policy communication. Critics cited her angry media interviews as an illustration of the perceived flaws in Corbyn's leadership team. Nonetheless, Abbott supported Corbyn's progressive platform, which included anti-austerity policies, the nationalization of vital industries, and foreign policy.

Public criticism and health issues: Abbott's health problems were revealed during the 2017 election campaign, prompting her to resign briefly as Shadow Home Secretary. She was eventually diagnosed with type 2 diabetes, which had worsened over the hectic campaign season. Abbott resumed work on June 18, 2017, following a brief rehabilitation period.

Abbott's role in the Labour Party changed dramatically after Jeremy Corbyn quit as leader in April 2020. She resigned as Shadow Home Secretary and was then nominated to the Home Affairs Select Committee.

Abbott has criticised Keir Starmer's leadership style and policy decisions on the party's orientation. Following the terrible local election results of May 2021, she told "The Guardian" that if Labour loses the Batley and Spen by-election, Starmer should retire. She also called the shadow cabinet shakeup, which included Angela Rayner's resignation, "baffling."

Position on the Ukraine Conflict: In February 2022, Abbott was one of eleven Labour MPs who signed the Stop the War Coalition's statement condemning the UK government's position on Ukraine's right to join NATO and calling on NATO to halt "eastward expansion." When faced with losing the whip, all eleven MPs, including Abbott, retracted their signatures.

Suspension and Restoration of the Labour Whip: In April 2023, Abbott submitted a letter to "The Observer" that was widely condemned for implying that Jews, Irish, and Travellers are less vulnerable to racism than black people. Following publication, Labour removed Abbott's whip, essentially suspending him from the parliamentary party. Abbott apologized, stating that her message was unintentionally distributed as a first draft. The whip was reintroduced in May 2024, following the completion of an online e-learning course. However, Abbott raised concern over the Labour leadership's treatment of her, alleging she was prevented from running as a Labour candidate in the 2024 general election, an allegation later refuted by party leader Keir Starmer.

Diane Abbott's time as Shadow Home Secretary was distinguished by her dedication to progressive ideas, unflinching support for Jeremy Corbyn, and perseverance in the face of widespread criticism and controversy. Throughout her career, she has been a strong advocate for social justice, equality, and human rights, always challenging the status quo inside her party and beyond. Despite health issues and political obstacles, Abbott has remained a prominent figure in British politics, exemplifying both the challenges and opportunities that minority women encounter in public life.

CONCLUSION

Diane Abbott is a groundbreaking figure in British politics, whose career has left an everlasting imprint on the public sector. She was born in London on September 27, 1953, into a family that instilled in her a strong belief in social justice and equality. Her rise from a young student at Harrow County Grammar School and Newnham College, Cambridge, to a famous Member of Parliament (MP) is truly extraordinary.

Abbott made history in 1987 as the first Black woman elected to the House of Commons, breaking barriers and setting a precedent for more diversity in British politics. Her election to represent Hackney North and Stoke Newington was a watershed moment, demonstrating her commitment to her community and capacity to solve complicated socioeconomic issues with empathy and intelligence.

Diane Abbott has been a prominent supporter of several issues throughout her career, including the struggle against racism, the promotion of equal opportunities, and the improvement of social welfare systems. Her dedication to these issues is demonstrated by her work on numerous parliamentary committees and active engagement in discussions about social justice, education, and healthcare.

Abbott's time in Parliament has not been without obstacles. She has undergone substantial criticism and opposition, but her fortitude and constancy demonstrate her commitment to public service. Her ability to manage the complexities of politics while remaining focused on the needs of her constituency demonstrates her leadership abilities.

Diane Abbott's influence extends beyond her political achievements to broader cultural issues. She has been an ardent advocate for tackling systemic injustices, and she has utilized her platform to bring attention to topics that might otherwise go unnoticed. Her contributions to public discourse have spurred critical discussions about race, identity, and justice, highlighting her status as a key figure in British politics and society.

Diane Abbott left a legacy of pioneering success and dedicated campaigning. Her career has not only paved the way for future generations of politicians, but it has also brought important topics to the forefront of public debate. As we consider her efforts, it is evident that Diane Abbott's influence stretches far beyond her legislative function; she is a symbol of tenacity, a champion of justice, and a crucial person in the continuous quest for a more equitable society. Her tale is a compelling reminder of how one individual can make a significant difference in the fight for social justice and a more inclusive world.

Printed in Great Britain
by Amazon